UNMASKING BULLYING IN SCHOOL

A Handbook for Students, Parents and Teachers

ROSE A. OKWANY-OGINGA

Dedication

To my family, friends and all who have contributed to my thoughts…

Table of Contents

vi

INTRODUCTION

THE TERM "BULLYING"

National Center against bullying (NCAB) defines bullying as a continuous process involving intentional cause of hurt, humiliation and harms to a victim who has difficulty stopping the behavior. Among students, bullying is perceived as a social or physical power based behavior. It is important noting that defining bullying varies greatly and may not be solely linked to the terminology but mostly the experience of the victims. Bullying not only has a negative impact on schools performance, it adversely affects communities we live in and students' freedom to learn in a safe and secure environment without fear.

Bullying is a wide spread phenomenon. For instance, in the United States

(US), bullying in schools is big problem for pupils and adolescents. Although people of all ages can be bullied, this phenomenon most often happens to school aged children. Sadly, it known over the years that bullying problem has grown in elementary, middle and high schools throughout America to a point that parents and school officials in most states have teamed up to stop bullying within US schools. Current reports suggest that, for every four students enrolled, one experiences regular bullying.

In Europe, Secondary schools in the United Kingdom (UK) experience the worst bullying compared to the rest of the schools in the region. 46% of secondary school pupils in the UK think that bullying is a problem in their schools. The UK bullying is largely attributed to students' language difficulties, race, skin color and religion. According to Taboola, Bullying in Chinese schools still experience traditional bullying irrespective of new emerging technological advances.

In Asia, bullying has been experienced in Chinese schools too. However, bullying in the China schools does not take place among the early ages of schooling (primary pupils and the secondary students) because these age groups are usually more busy with their learning activities and are being more watched by the teachers in schools and family members at home. Moreover, at this stage most children are concerned about the rules and regulations that fall upon them from their school and family.

In Africa, highest bullying trends is experienced in Kenyan schools compared to other countries within the continent. A study found out that 82% of Kenyan students had their belongings taken away from them by bullies, 63% were physically assaulted and 64% had been blackmailed or

2

threatened. Therefore, it is worth noting that bullying is an everlasting problem internationally and is mainly administered by older students to their vulnerable pray. Bullying is rife at South African schools too. Memoh's publication in 2013 revealed the frequency of bullying amongst high school learners to be 36% in Cape Town and 41% at national level of the total number of high school learners. Moreover, bullying behavior in schools has been found to lead to problems such as a low self-esteem, low academic performance, absenteeism, depression, and consequently school dropout in African countries.

To summarize, bullied students often develop concentration problems and continue to have learning difficulties. This hampers efforts to raise educational standards and improve schools around the world. Additionally, there is a vicious cycle of bully/victim relationships that negatively influence on individual learners. It is therefore vital to explore and expose the causes of bullying, create awareness and address issues related to bullying and to make victims or "future victims" have an idea of identifying bullies, what do and how to avoid being targeted.

OBJECTIVES OF THIS BOOK

This review handbook will help a parent, teacher or student to;

❖ Understand the extent, seriousness, and dynamics of bullying and further recognize and respond early and effectively to behaviors that will lead to bullying.

❖ Prepare students to respond effectively to early bullying behavior by creating a society where students understands that bullying behaviors.

❖ Empower students to actively intervene to prevent and stop bullying, expose bullying in schools, and explore causes of bullying among children and adolescents in the middle school and High School.

❖ To act as a guide in helping with effective strategies to control bullying among children and adolescents in middle school and High School.

BULLY IDENTIFICATION, HOW TO BE PREPARED

BULLYING POLICY

Zero tolerance policy relies on exclusionary measures such as suspension and expulsion whenever a bullying has been reported. However, most schools around the world are trying to curb the push out problem by implementing the Positive Behavior Support (PBS) instead of zero tolerance policy. PBS is data driven, an evidence-based approach proven to reduce disciplinary incidents, increase a school's sense of safety, improve attendance rate and support improved outcomes. Conversely, zero tolerance measures have a long time negative consequences since it does not solve the problem of the bully, who typically spends more unsupervised time at home or in the community. Moreover, Zero tolerance policy approach can result in a high level of suspensions without full comprehension of how the behavior needs to and can be changed. PBS policy therefore helps reduce bullying incidences or causes in schools.

WHAT ARE THE TYPES OF BULLYING?

According to Bullying.gov, bullying is packaged in many ways. A search for types of bullying over the net yields about 230 million results. Upon review of different pages and articles ((Duncan 1999, Freedman 2002, Guillain 2011, Hanson-Harding 2013, Doering 2016), I herein summarize the common types of bullying experienced in learning institutions:

Physical Bullying

Physical bullying involves striking, punching, pinching, pushing, kicking, making mean or rude hand gestures, tripping and spitting on other children and students (Rivkin 2013, Higgins 2016). It also includes damaging someone's belongings. Physical bullying is very easy identifying as a result, it is most likely what people think of when they think of bullying. This form of bullying has historically received more attention from schools than other forms of bullying.

Verbal Bullying

This is the most common type among students (Rivkin, 2013). It includes perpetuating rumors and use of derogatory terms and obscenities, which targets learners according to their gender, race, religion, culture and sexual orientation(Rivkin 2013). Verbal bullying includes name-calling, insults, homophobic or racist remarks and verbal abuse. Therefore, it is noteworthy that bullying goes beyond the physical abuse and verbal abuse is as harmful as physical bullying. The goal of verbal bullies is to degrade and demean the victim, while making the aggressor look dominant and powerful. However bullies tend to focus on creating a situation in which the aggressor dominates the victim. And this can happen verbally as well as physically.

Generally, girls prefer this form as compared to boys. In addition to verbal bullying, girls tend to use social exclusion techniques, to dominate others and show their superiority and power. Taken together, this form of bullying is implemented among students or adolescents to avoid trouble of getting into physical confrontation. Verbal bullying affects one's self image, emotions and psychological development. Moreover, it contributes to low self-esteem, as well as depression and other problems. It can aggravate problems that a victim may already be experiencing at home or in other places. In some cases, verbal bullying can reach a point where the victim is depressed, and wants to develop suicidal thoughts. Additionally, students resort to substance abuse or in some extreme cases suicide. In the end, words have a power all their own, and the realities of verbal bullying can have very physical consequences, even if the bully never lays a finger on the victim. It remains a challenge for teachers and school administration to detect verbal bullying since no physical harm takes place. Parents should therefore be of what is goes on in your child's life, and be a place that he or she can turn if verbal bullying is occurring. It is therefore important that parents be aware of the reluctance of their children to go to school, complaints that no one likes him or her, prolonged depression, a drop in school performance or drastic changes in eating and sleeping patterns since these factors constitutes some signs that a student might be a victim of insults from verbal bullies

Sexual Bullying

This consists of repeated, harmful, and humiliatory actions that target a person sexually

(Duncan 1999). The harm and humiliation comes in the form of crude comments, name calling, vulgar gestures, uninvited touching include sexual name-calling, propositioning and use of pornographic materials. Comment deemed sexual come in the flavor of a girl's appearance, attractiveness, sexual development, or sexual activity. In extreme cases, sexual bullying opens the door to sexual assault.

This bullying is mostly administered by males who mostly often targeting girls. These mostly start via sex texting as friends but when the advances as stopped results in sexual bullying. An instance is when girl shares photo of herself to a boyfriend and when there is a break up, the boyfriend shares that photo with the entire school. In the end, she becomes the target of sexual bullying because people make fun of her body, call her crude names, and make vulgar comments about her. Most boys depict this as open invitation to proposition her or sexually assault the girl.

Cyber Bullying

Bullying through internet means is referred to as "cyber bullying" (Scherer, 2015, Campbell and Bauman, 2018). This is a type of bullying where people post embarrassing comments targeting someone or his/her images on the

Internet. Cyber bullying is experience worldwide due to the technological advances and access to free home or institutional internet. This gives learner's access to social media pages, which facilitates bullying in and out of schools. It can also refer to the use of technology for example email, mobile telephones, chat rooms, social networking sites. Bullying, once restricted to the school environment, has now moved into the Internet (Trolley and Hanel 2010).

The current trend is, children or teenagers desire to connect with friends using different unmonitored applications. School going kids and teenagers are not only owning tablets, gaming devices, and mobile phones at a younger age, they also want access to popular social media sites, and the ability to engage in online games and share information (Giant 2013).

Since these generation of children spend unmonitored time playing with friends and engaging with each other in the cyberworld, "talking" with each other, "talking" to each other, and "talking" about each other, often without adult or parental monitoring, this fuels the aspect of cyber bullies (Scheinbaum 2018). While technology allows this generation of school going children to connect in meaningful ways, such as the opportunity to share ideas, photos, videos, and more, the unsupervised nature of the internet leads to high degree of cyber bullying that is translated to verbal when they decide to attack one another without their gadgets in schools. Use of Internet among school going children should therefore be guided and restrictions put in place (Campbell and Bauman 2018).

Social Emotional Bullying

Social emotional bullying involves groups of children and adolescents, excluding other children and other adolescents in their activities and in their conversations in an attempt to make them feel very uncomfortable and insecure about themselves. It also includes lying, spreading rumors, playing a nasty joke and mimicking

Prejudicial Bullying

This type of bullying is based on prejudices teens have toward people of different race, religion, or sexual orientation. Prejudicial bullying can embrace all the other types of bullying. This is commonly witnessed when children or teens single out others who are different from them. This type of bullying is often severe and can open the door to hate crimes.

CHARACTERISCTICS OF BULLIES

In academic environment, bullies vary from one person to another. They have different styles, personalities, goals, and behaviors. And their motivations for and methods of bullying are all different. Bullies fall into several categories and some may appear to be in a category of their own. Below is review (Carter 2015) of different types of bullies commonly experiences in school premises.

Bully Victims

This constitutes the group that was once bullied (Carter, 2015). They target weaker victims than them because they, too, have been bullied. Their goal usually is to regain a sense of power and control in their lives. This type of bully is very common. Most teens and children who bully others have been bullied themselves. Their bullying is a way of retaliating for the pain they are feeling. Some bully victims come from a home riddled with domestic violence or suffers abuse from an older sibling in which case, bullying is a learned behavior.

The main characteristic of this group is that they are loners or fall at the bottom of the social ladder at school. This motivates them and fuels the sense of powerlessness and anger they feel. Consequently, their bullying often appears hostile, which can cause the bully to be unpopular. This in turn perpetuates the cycle of the bully victim.

Popular Bullies

It is widely accepted that these are the big ego brothers and sisters in schools. They are characterized to have a group of followers or feels like they rule the school. Moreover, popular bullies have a sense of entitlement that can stem from their popularity, their size, their upbringing or their socio-economic status. They thrive on the physical power and control they have over their victims and may boast about their bullying. Their preferred mode of administering their act is via physical acts like pushing around, taking their books or pinning them against lockers. Unlike boys in this category, popular girls use relational aggression. They spread rumors, are manipulative, and often exclude others.

Most of these bullies thrive on the attention and power they get from bullying since they are star athlete or perceived school leaders. Since this is happens mostly among the teens, other teens often tolerate this type of bully because they would rather be accepted than bullied.

Relational Bullies

These are the group of popular students that enjoy deciding who is accepted at school and who isn't. They exclude, isolate, and ostracize to execute their tactics. Most relational bullies will use only verbal or emotional bullying to maintain control. Relational bullies also maintain their power by using rumors, gossip, labels, and name-calling. They target others because of jealousy or self-conclusion of being socially unacceptable. Maintaining popularity is the key reason for relational aggression.

Serial Bullies

These bullies are systematic, controlled, and calculated in their approach. They represent an image of sweet, charming, and charismatic to authoritative figures. Contrary, they can be cold and calculating and tend to inflict emotional pain on their victims over long periods of time. More than often, serial bullies use physical bullying but only if they can be sure they won't be caught. These bullies are skilled manipulators and liars and are usually fake friends. Their sweet and nice persona is just another way to manipulate situations to their liking. When confronted with trouble, they are capable of twisting facts and situations to make them look innocent. Serial bullies are often so skilled at deception that their victims often are afraid to speak up, convinced that no one will ever believe them.

Group Bullies

These are typically part of a group and have a pack mentality when they are together. They bully as a group but behave much differently when they are alone even if they are alone with the victim. These guys have a leader whom individual members of the group imitate the leader of the group and just follow along. Because young people "bullies" feel insulated when they are in a group, they often feel free to say and do things they wouldn't do otherwise. They also feel less responsibility for their actions because "they are working in a group."

Indifferent Bullies

This is the group that has no or unable to feel empathy. Therefore they are characterized to often appear cold, unfeeling, and detached and have very little, if any, remorse for what they do to others. These bullies, although less common than the other types of bullies, are often the most dangerous. They bully victims for the enjoyment of seeing another person suffer. Indifferent bullies are not deterred by <u>disciplinary consequences.</u> Furthermore, indifferent bullies are often vicious and have deep psychological problems that need to be addressed professionally. And bullying interventions does not usually bring about change in their actions.

CAUSES OF BULLYING

In 2005, Hibbert Adam published a book asking the question, "Why do people bully (Hibbert 2005)". It is important to note that the frequency and severity of bullying is related to lack of adult supervision received by a child in the home and negative actions are intentional attempts to injure or cause discomfort in others. Personal experience as an African American, born and brought up in native Africa, bullying stigmatizes the peers and may cause serious psychological problems if not detected and addressed. There are several factors that contribute to bullying among pupils and adolescents (Beane 2008). Peer pressure, indiscipline, drug/ substance abuse, harsh punishment from teachers, unclear defined procedure in administration of students' discipline, disciplinary measures such as denying students' rights to meals are some of the factors that negatively influence students to engage in bullying.

Peer pressure

This is the pressure from others to conform to the attitudes, behaviors and personal habits of a group. When peers spend time together, they influence one another positively or negatively this is because they learn from each other (Sherri, 2016). According to Sherri, children and adolescence give in to peer pressure just because they want to be liked or fit in and at the same time they have fear that if they do not go along with the group or clique, then other peers might make fun of them, as a result bullying sometimes is an act of self-preservation (Sherri, 2016).

Indiscipline

Indiscipline is one of the major problems that basically affect schools negatively. Learners who are indiscipline are often uncontrollable and always do as they wish. Indiscipline affects school and home environment and as a result fighting among children and ill-behavior becomes the order of the day leading to various bullying experiences among peers

Drug/Substance Abuse

Most pupils and adolescents who take drugs at school or at home become violent and will automatically violate other learners' rights. This can also lead to fights between learners thereby allowing them to bully other peers. Harsh punishment from teachers

Consequences of these harsh disciplinary practices like suspension and expulsion are devastating. Children and adolescents who are repeatedly suspended or who are expelled, are more likely to fall behind their peers academically paving way to their eventual drop out or acquisition of behaviors that lead to bullying practices.

Unclear Defined Procedure in Administration of Students' Discipline

Some teachers and administrators create a sense of hopelessness among students when they call for law enforcement for disciplinary matters for which they use to call home and also help to resolve conflict leaving the officers to arrest students making the consequences devastating. This has led to bullying is schools as students are not ready for such kind of procedures and they therefore develop unwanted characters

Disciplinary Measures Such As Denying Students' Rights to Meals

This is another cause of bullying in schools. When children are denied their rights as a disciplinary measure, they tend to behave differently and it can sometimes lead to indiscipline cases causing bullying to take place in the school set up. All indiscipline cases must be punished using correct measure.

EFFECTS OF BULLYING

Bullying is perceived as a form of social interaction that many school children experience. Children and adolescents, who are involved in different types of bullying, are at risk of poor school functioning, as measured by academic performance, attitudes toward school and absenteeism (Bodenstein, Potterton et al. 2002, Garrett 2003, Rivers, Duncan et al. 2007, Herweck 2017, Osanloo, Reed et al. 2017). Some of the effects of bullying in primary and high schools are manifested in many ways and they include violence, high school dropout rates of children and adolescents and low self-esteem (Bodenstein, Potterton et al. 2002). Those with serious psychosocial problems in schools might experience problems associated with attention, behavior, and emotion regulation, which interfere with their ability to learn. According to Afro and Shafqat, Children and adolescents being bullied or suffering from any peer mistreatment show low academic achievements than the non-bullied peers' students who report a better rapport with their teachers and other students.

Bullying among learners not only decreases their academic performance but also cause mental health problems and physical injury. Learners may suffer significant psychological distress and in rare instances take their own life. Bullying therefore may lead to suicidal tendencies in school aged groups or victims. A study performed or done by Yale University shows that children and adolescents who are bullied by other peers consider suicide than those who are not bullied. Elementary school children who are bullied often miss school more and drop out of school than those who are not bullied. The study continues to reveal that as the bullied children become older; they end up committing acts such as theft, vandalism, truancy, and fighting.

It is therefore believed that victims or bullied children and adolescents live in a state of anger, they are depressed, stressed and even learn helplessness. They feel insecure, lack trust and sometimes very sensitive to situations and experience personality disorder. Learners who bully their peers become uncontrollable and at the same time very difficult to manage leading to time wastage during conflict resolution meetings instead of carrying on with the normal routine which is teaching and learning.

SOLUTION TO BULLYING

It is no secret that bullying is a wide spread social issue that impacts the quality of education of young learners who should be aware if they are being abused(Gordon 2016). Bullying preventions programs and strategies seek to improve peer relations and make schools safe and positive places for students to learn and develop. School's teachers should plan for strategies that can reduce bullying among children and adolescents in middle school and high school. Successful bullying prevention strategy and intervention should also consider all the factors that can facilitate active involvement of families and the community. Some of the interventions to reduce bullying can be:

Parental Involvement/Support

Proper parental support can be a protective factor for bullying. Parents can also detect and manage bullying. For crucial eradication of bullying in schools, Parent-Teacher partnership is vital in all areas. Parental involvement is where parents develop a plan to address bullying among children and adolescents. They seek a face to face meeting with the students' teachers, year level coordinators, deputy principals and principals to discuss the bullying issues among children. Parents need to step up to the challenge of bullying and talk to their children, give ideas on how to respond to and deal with peer pressure and establish different rules and the necessary consequences when it comes to bullying (Gordon 2016). Parents are also expected to be calm during the meeting sessions, bring evidences they have, record minutes of the meeting and create a record of what has been agreed upon in order to address the bullying issues and find solutions to bullying in the school.

Peer Support Initiative

This involves trained students offering support to others. Schools set good examples by creating a sense of responsibility among individuals by motivating them to help their peer's distress. Training should also be provided for teachers, administrators and other school staff so that they can recognize and respond to bullying and learn intervention strategies.

Conflict Resolution

This is a form of conflict resolution which involves a mediated meeting between the victim and offender aimed at making them understand the harmful effects of their actions, the unacceptable nature of their behavior and the development of a monitored plan to remediate the situation.

Integration Of Anti-Bullying Themes Into The Curriculum

This involves integration of the anti-bullying activities and discussion related to bullying in the curriculum. Teachers play a central role in the way bullying policies and programs are presented and delivered to learners. Curriculum intervention is a critical component of anti-bullying programs because students learn how to stand up to bullies and assist victims.

Shared concerned method

This is an approach based on the assumption that bullies typically are insensitive to the harm they are doing to the victim. This is because of their involvement in a group which gives legitimacy to bullying, reducing their sense of personal responsibility. This model uses the fact that bullies commonly feel uncomfortable with their own behavior. An adult mediator uses specific techniques to demonstrate the impact of bullying on the victim. Although the method involves a no blaming approach, it does not seek to excuse or condone bullying and has been found to be effective in many setting.

Creation of Clear Anti-Bullying Rules and Policies

This is the formulation of anti-bullying policies that ensures that members of staff handle incidences associated with bullying consistently. If a school has understood rules of conduct and fair disciplinary practices, they will report less violence.

Peer Student Support

Peer medication is a process in which students resolve disputes and conflict among their peers. Peer mediators are chosen by their own peers and receive training to work with both the bully and the victim to arrive at a nonaggressive, constructive solution. It has been used successfully with children in a number of school settings

Campaigns

These are platforms created by victims where they give and share their experiences on what they have gone through. This can help those who have suffered and especially the parents whose children have gone through bullying to avoid suffering at all times.

Early Detection

Early detection of bullying is also a solution to bullying. Given the high prevalence of bullying, screening routine is appropriate or suitable with every child or adolescence in school environment and home environment. This gives an opportunity for the teachers to deal with the issues immediately.

Online Resources

These are website created and maintained by different organizations. They provides a database of anti-bullying materials and the required initiatives, tips for dealing with a variety of difficult situations in life, and testimonials from the known and unknown people who overcame bullying.

Cooperative Group Work

These are groups created in class to help the children manage different task within the teaching and learning sessions. Within the group, each and every member is responsible for a given task. This helps to reduce idleness and at the same time group members are able to assist their peers, correct the unwanted behavior and appreciate all the members. Working together creates safety and orderliness in the classrooms and the same time it would help the learners to spent time on instruction and not on ineffective activities.

CONCLUSION

Bullying is a serious problem faced in many schools across the world. Effective bullying prevention programs help to make schools safe and positive places for children and adolescents to learn and interact with their peers. Moreover, bullying is emerging as a significant but preventable mental health risk factor for young people. This handbook summarizes information from different cited resources that will be beneficial to parent, teachers and students as they pursue their studies while being potentially targeted by their peers.

Summary

Bullying is an unending problem mostly experienced by school going children in learning institutions and neighborhoods. This phenomenon is practiced at all levels of education beginning from the early ages of learning to the universities. Bullying is perceived to be a power-based problem that lasts forever in the lives of students. Therefore, creation of bullying awareness is critical in understanding and dealing with this vice schools. Limiting these advances are the unanswered questions whether the victims, teachers and parents have a basic understanding or aware of bullying in learning institutions, whether school administration diagnoses and guard victims from bully victimization? And whether rebellious student's behaviors depend on the nature of unreported bullying they endure? This books therefore aims to present a simplified review of bullying in schools; enable student, teachers and parents identify bullying behavior, the bully, the victim and the complicit bystander. Furthermore, the book explores strategies for preventing, combating, deescalating and resolving bullying.

REFERENCES

Afroz, J., & Shafqat, H. (2015). Bullying in the elementary schools: Its causes and effects on students. Journal of education and Practice, 6.

Blazer, C. (2005, March). Literature Review on bullying.

Brownstein, R. (2009). Teaching Tolerance: Discipline and behavior.

Carr-Gregg, M., & Manocha, R. (2011). Bullying: Effects,Prevalence and Strategies for detection. Australia.

Einarsen, S. (1999). The nature and causes of bullying at work. International Journal of Manpower.

Lipset, A. (2008). UK Schools worst in Europe for Bullying.

Mwangi, J. K. (2013). Factors contributing to bullying among students in Public Secondary Schools in Kiambu District in Kenya.

Ngesa, L. M., Gunga, S., Wachira, L., Muriithi, E., & K'Odhiambo, K. A. (2013). Bullying in Kenyan Secondary Schools: Manifestation, Causes, Consequences and Mitigation Measures. Nairobi.

Odengo, R. (2007). Bullying in Kenya. Nairobi.

Sherri, G. (2016). How peer pressure can lead to bullying: How to help your kids cope with peer pressure.

Sherri, G. (2016). School Bullying Prevention: An overview of bullying prevention programms.

Taboola. (2015, December 22). Bullying in China.

Taboola. (2015). Bullying in the United States of America.

Taboola. (2015, December 22). Bullying in the United States of America.

Tine, L. M., Helena, S. N., & Simonsen, M. (2012). The Effects of Bullying in Elementary Schools. Germany.

Vumumzi, N. N., & Almon, S. (2013). The nature, causes and effects of school violence in South Africa. South Africa Journal of Education.

Beane, A. L. (2008). Protect your child from bullying : expert advice to help you recognize, prevent, and stop bullying before your child gets hurt. San Francisco, CA, Jossey-Bass.

Bodenstein, M., M. Potterton and Catholic Institute of Education (South Africa) (2002). Stop it! : a guide to dealing with abuse in schools. Johannesburg, Catholic Institute of Education.

Campbell, M. and S. Bauman (2018). Reducing cyberbullying in schools : international evidence-based best practices. London, Academic Press, an imprint of Elsevier.

Carter, S. (2015). The hostile environment : students who bully in school. Lanham, Maryland, Lexington Books.

Doering, A. F. (2016). Insults aren't funny : what to do about verbal bullying. North Mankato, Minnesota, Capstone.

Duncan, N. (1999). Sexual bullying : gender conflict and pupil culture in secondary schools. London ; New York, Routledge.

Freedman, J. S. (2002). Easing the teasing : helping your child cope with name-calling, ridicule, and verbal bullying. Chicago, Contemporary Books.

Garrett, A. G. (2003). Bullying in American schools : causes, preventions, interventions. Jefferson, N.C., McFarland & Co.

Giant, N. (2013). E-safety for the i-generation : combating the misuse and abuse of technology in schools. London ; Philadelphia, Jessica Kingsley Publishers.

Gordon, S. M. (2016). Are you being abused? New York, NY, Enslow Publishing.

Guillain, C. (2011). Coping with bullying. Chicago, Ill., Heinemann Library.

Hanson-Harding, A. (2013). How to beat physical bullying. New York, NY, Rosen Central.

Herweck, D. (2017). Safe & sound : stop bullying. Huntington Beach, CA, Teacher Created Materials.

Hibbert, A. (2005). Why do people bully? Chicago, Ill., Raintree. Higgins, M. (2016).

Pushing isn't funny : what to do about physical bullying. North Mankato, Minn., Capstone Picture Window Books, a Capstone Imprint.

Osanloo, A. F., C. J. Reed and J. P. Schwartz (2017). Creating and negotiating collaborative spaces for socially just anti-bullying interventions for K-12 schools. Charlotte, NC, Information Age Publishing, Inc. Rivers, I., N. Duncan and V. E.

Besag (2007). Bullying : a handbook for educators and parents. Westport, Conn., Praeger.

Rivkin, J. (2013). Physical bullying. New York, Crabtree Publishing Company.

Rivkin, J. (2013). Verbal bullying. St. Catherines, ON ; New York, NY, Crabtree Publishing Company.

Scheinbaum, A. C. (2018). The dark side of social media : a consumer psychology perspective. New York, Routledge.

Scherer, L. S. (2015). Cyberbullying. Farmington Hills, Mich., Greenhaven Press, a part of Gale, Cengage Learning.

Trolley, B. and C. Hanel (2010). Cyber kids, cyber bullying, cyber balance. Thousand Oaks, Calif., Corwin Press.

About the Author

Rose A. Okwany-Oginga has a Master of Science degree in leadership from Grand Canyon University, Arizona, a Bachelor of Education degree from University of Nairobi, Kenya, and two Associate degrees: one in nursing from Breckenridge Nursing School and the other in liberal arts from Hillsborough Community College in Florida. She currently works as a nurse in Tampa, Florida. In addition, she is the founder and CEO of IHOPEE (International Health Operations Patients Education and Empowerment), an organization that equips youth and women in the USA and Kenya through education and life skills to face challenges with hope in health and economic matters, building partnerships through www.ihopee.com. She serves as a leader in many youth and women organizations mentoring and coaching career development and networking through Certified ILV (ideal life Vision). She is regularly called upon to provide training to various groups within schools and the broader community in Florida area and beyond.

The professional writing she has accomplished is based on her fifteen years of experience teaching and a passion for reading with a dedication to lifelong learning.. Never to waste any time she spends a lot of time with her family. She has four great children. She volunteers services as a Rotarian in Florida. Acting as a nurse is a means through which she is able to act as a humble servant leader on a daily basis. Both spiritually and intellectually her mission is to return the blessings she has received from the Lord.

CPSIA information can be obtained
at www.ICGtesting.com
Printed in the USA
LVHW072254080919
630364LV00013B/614/P